HIDE AND SEEK

Poems by
Vernon Daniel

1998

First Impression—September 1998

ISBN 1 85902 697 4

© Vernon Daniel

All rights reserved. No part of this book may be reproduced, stored in a retrieval system, or transmitted in any form or by any means, electronic, electrostatic, magnetic tape, mechanical, photocopying, recording or otherwise, without permission in writing from the author.

*Printed in Wales by
Gomer Press, Llandysul, Ceredigion*

MILKY WAY

A brilliance
dwindles in dark.
And we are no more
than shadows
on a cosmic wheel
that makes
and puts out stars.

This book is dedicated
to my parents: the past;
and the future:
Hilary and Guy.

CONTENTS

Milky Way

Rivulet	13
Sansevieria	15
Shell	16
Egg	18
The Green Fuse	19
Aquamarine	20
Brood	21
Formation	22
Bumble Bee	23
Aspects	24
Kestrel	26
Onlooker	27
I will sing praises	28
Pheasant	30
Hedgehog	31
Weasel	32
Options	34
Britons	36
Salome	38
Rome	41
Julius Caesar	42
Pompeii	43
Heroine	44
The Keep	46
The Tribe	48
Polynesian	50
Winchester College	51
Venice	52

Contents *(continued)*

Landing	54
Florentine	56
Inventor	58
Vulcan	60
Forecast: Constant	62
Village	64
Co-ordinates	66
Nursery Lines	67
Hide and Seek	69
Caravan	71
Meeting	72
Heatherbank	74
The Hailstones	76
Recorded	77
San Michele	78
An Art Deco Shop	80
Movies	82
Limelight	84
Saturnalia	85
Crowd	86
Metropolis III	87
Metropolis IV	88
Still Life	90
Alms	91
Busker	92
One is a lonely number	93
Certainly	94
Co op.	95
Preference	96

Contents *(continued)*

Ciao	97
Snap	98
Utility	99
Cressida	100
Umbrella	101
Not merely being, becoming	103
Aphrodite	104
Hotel Ariele	105
Absence	107
Waitress	108
In the twinkle of an eye	109
Haiku	110
Name Dropping	111
Surreal	113
Instanter	115
Score	117
Expressivo	118
Silence	120
Prospect	121
Firmament	122
Pyre	124
Adjuration	125
Recurrence	126
Solar	127

RIVULET*

The clouds
drift
in blue,
darken
and break
into rain
fall
on mountain sides.

The pure water
trickles
through gorse and reed
trips
over gravel, sand
slips
into spring.
Fern fronds, leaves

float
down stream
blessing the terrain
touching the rough edge
with clarity.
The notes
splash down
on a score for sand,

a lyric for immersed pebbles.
The light
plays
on gold, ruby sapphire.

* On hearing the last four songs of Richard Strauss.

Silver light
reflects
each curviture.
As cool as marble,

sheep
place
their tongues in water.
To the lark's pointed beak,
the rippling
is the voice of things
syllabic:
the language of the reeds.

And further down stream
forms
a water fall
cascading
on the rocks below
splashing the air
meandering

to river
flowing
to the sea,
to be changed
caressed by warmth
made weightless
raised
to cloud.

SANSEVIERIA*

On the isle
of Madagascar,
this plant
was first seen
by the odd adventurer
and marvelled at
by botanists

giving it
an exotic name.
In its upward thrust,
points like a cluster
of blades.
Its posture
twisting

fingering the air.
Its texture smooth,
a tropic green
mottled black
with yellow rim.
In dramatic form,
each rigid leaf

curves
promoting
its protective purpose.
From the dark infusion
of soil, heat and rain
a tiny, white flower
comes.

* a succulent, related to the cacti.

SHELL

I must
write words
for this shell
(its gene
is as good
as it gets).

For here
in air,
a silence
underlines
the sand
beneath.

A surface
as smooth
as marble;
the underpart
delicately
pink.

This is
elaborate
carapace:
the size
tried
and changed

pushed
to the rim.
The texture
rocklike
is itself
colourful

to grace
the sound
of seabed:
a sculpture
to be
reckoned with.

Egg

Reptilian
    rim
   eliptical
   curving
    form
    moving
    pliably
     from
      soft
   feathered
   warmth.
   In air,
     it
  hardens
  heading
 for light
emerges
shell
cracking.

THE GREEN FUSE*

In the blue
or green of it,
the genetic strains
conjoin.

Couples
oscillate
pulsate
erupt
inseminate
gestate.

With Lucina*
forcing
all creatures
into being
becoming
themselves
particularly
in the blue
and green of it.

---

* The force that through the green fuse drives the flower.
                                                    Thomas
** Lucina: Roman goddess of light and birth.

AQUAMARINE

On islands palmed
to hide the sun,
fishermen waded
out to sea.

Waist high
a net was thrown
to catch the fish
with bare hands:

fish as bright
as silver
in a sea of green.

Frantic birds
flocked and fluttered
sunlight blushed
a cloud along.

A prize held
between the palms
convulsed
to stillness:

fish as strange
as crystal
from a sea of green.

BROOD

The water flows
effortlessly
taking them
down stream.

The ducklings scurry
they must keep up.
The mallard feels
there's safety

in numbers
(eleven eggs
unforgettably
hatched).

Does it know
the broods
compelling number?
Some will always

push, push to the rim
and then an alarm,
an egalitarian
concern

an intensified
quack! quack!
to keep them
intact.

FORMATION

Their necks stretch in body line.

The mallards flap and skim

over the roof tiles.

Quacking is heard.

Water reeds

call.

BUMBLE BEE

It was on
the sill
close

to
my eyes
more rounded

more
itself
with its black

garb,
yellow
certainty

bare.
The wings
still . . . tiny,

but
the buzz
was missing.

ASPECTS

1.   A crystal wave
the dragon-fly will ride
the lapping and lurking
of tired tides.
The webbed wing
the wind is spreading.

Wind and rain
and sea applaud.
Foaming and rolling,
moving and falling
the spectre fine
with watery wing.

On tiny eyes
the sand will shine
while curled and coloured
shells will sing
of all the fun and joy it brings.

2.   Aesthetically,
it is a matter
of the right
distance
from an object
such as watching
a dragon-fly
hovering
above the water
balletlike.

In close up,
this dragon
has voracious
real jaws
and the closer
the victims get
(like those tiny midges)
sees
this beauty turn
to viciousness.

KESTREL

A child brought it
in a cardboard box,
found it stark
in a dry hedge.
This kestrel killed
a rodent, mole or shrew
riddled with insecticide.
Fatally struck
as a doomed knight,

its tail was paralized.
Vicelike the tallons clasped.
The wings stretched and flapped.
To see such beauty flexed
for flight, then turn
somersault in helplessness.
We placed it in a tree
forked for tournament.
It fell to the ground

humiliated, clutching
its own dignity,
To see the creature
struggle with itself
(no ground cry had a pitch
as high as this).
Then close to earth
where strange shapes scream,
folds its wings for good.

ONLOOKER

From the little boat,
I could see that
at a distant time
a convulsion split
the headland shaping
the island,* cutting
a rock face stiff
with limestone
that touched the sea
precipitously.

From a vantage point,
a solitary seagull
looks down intrigued
(by the noise
of the outboard motor
and a little boat
in a choppy sea)
as if to say
wherever you are going to,
I have already been.

* Capri.

I WILL SING PRAISES

To wild horses
in soft meadows,
I will sing praises
to agile pumas
on rocky crags,
scurrying lizards
in mean deserts
and loud macaws
on tropic palms.

To herds of bison
in vast prairies,
I will sing praises
to shiny cormorants
diving hard,
green, green frogs
in dappled pools
to bedraggled wolves
in forests cold.

To serious goats
in high sierras,
I will sing praises
to velvet moles
underground,
to gaudy snakes
in stoney warmth
and turtles pushing
into sand.

To green insects
on silvery boughs,
I will sing praises
to monkeys screaming
on a dying branch,
to grotesque fish
in heavy shoals
and tigers
in the long grass.

PHEASANT

It happened
on a quiet
country road.
A pheasant
was hit by
an oncoming
car.

Irrevocably
hurt,
it tried hard,
fitfully
to push its way
out of itself.
After this

dance of death,
I placed it
like a still,
warm cushion
on the soft
green bank
and left.

HEDGEHOG

Curled
defensively,
the face was pointed
safely
to the spines.

It woke up
and sniffed round.
Like clockwork
it shuffled
through the grass.

I read somewhere
that they were
flea ridden;
a paltry thing
to say of any

creature,
pushing
with snout and spikes
searching out
the snails and slugs.

WEASEL

The name of weasel
may bring to mind
a comic song
or a dubious character
in an Edgar Wallace yarn.

The real weasel
is rarely seen
undulating through
the long grass.
A lithesome carnivore,

weighs
a quarter of a pound
with delicate claws
and fur a chestnut brown.
This small cousin

of the stoat
penetrates
the narrowest burrow.
With rounded head
poised to the rodent scent,

bites the vertebrae
incisevly
below the neck.
Catlike, takes the prey
to open nest,

a rotting trunk
or hole in bank.
Wesle
the old English word
sounds so inappropriate

for one that wriggles
from the talons
of the hawk
and bounds to such
decisive ends.

OPTIONS
(or existential angst)

They have flown their cote
for an adventurous season
or released for cost or mere
boredom. They fly round this house
and grace the air above the trees,
    between earth and sky:
    an aesthetic brilliance.
    A white magnificence,
    the pigeon changed into
    a cooing angel and from
the pairing, a sustained bond,
a potent symbol, ritually
released in droves
to pure radiance.
On the other wing, there is
    nesting and breeding and the droppings
    and the clawing, the noise.
    This shadow is part of the real scene.
    Such is impingement and the experts say
    there are four options, to seal
the fate of the doves. The first
you leave them as they are
and they will multiply
and all else will multiply.
The second is to send them away
    for a short while from the eaves,
    then shut off the entrance to the nest.
    Up there, they will still relate
    to this roof for this is
    their chosen site.

The third is more accommodating
by placing a dove cote, free standing
in the grounds and place them
in their new home—not an easy task
for they may not approve.
    You must feed them with seed
    and water for many weeks,
    a commitment that may not succeed.
    The fourth and last is ethically
    questionable, a drastic, final
solution: you put them down
like so much vermin, for words
are flexible and we give to them
the meaning we approve, as a reason
to rid us of an impingement:
    a relating, a blessing
    or annoyance and aversion
    In the chosen silence
    enchantment fades
    and guilt is borne.

BRITONS

The Welsh
have been going west

ever since
the Romans came,

placing Celtic names
like stepping stones:

Jenkins and Owen,
Lewis and Harris,

Morgan and Roberts,
Thomas and Morris,

Rowlands and James,
Howells and Hughes,

Richards and Vaughan,
Evans and Pugh,

Davies and Jones,
Griffiths and Rees,

Williams and John,
Powell and Price,

Pritchard, Edwards,
and those Llewellyns

stepping down
(conjugating

those Latin verbs)
to coracles

crossing the Afon.*

---

* Welsh for river.

SALOME*
(a tragic tale)

Time was just before the first millennium.
The place was Galilee, a Roman province,
governed by Herod, the Tetrarch.** A Hebrew
prophet known as John*** (forever talking of a
Messiah, Judgement Day, atonement and
apocalypse) condemned Herod for his marriage
to his brother's wife, comparing her to a
serpent of iniquity, giving herself up
under the lust of her eyes.

Herod was affronted by his stark rhetoric
and to still his voice, imprisoned him.

Salome, Herod's daughter-in-law, intrigued
by this prophet, asked the guard to bring
him forth
that she might see and talk to him for herself.
She found that he had a captivating voice,
eyes as fiery as a torch, wasted body
but straight as an ivory statue. He who had
survived the desert, clothed roughly in
camel hair,
eating locusts and honey. She was entranced
with the body white like the lilies of the field
or the rose of the Queen of Sheba. Strong he
was but gentle.

---

* On hearing the opera by Richard Strauss with the libretto by Oscar Wilde.
** governor
*** John the Baptist

Salome was charismatic, desirable,
undefiled and as pure as the moon is blue.
She referred to his hair as black as the night.

You are the daughter of Sodom, for by woman
came evil into the world. You must wash your
sins away in the purity of a stream.

She described his lips as a scarlet band,
as red as the feet of those who tread the grape.

He spoke of an invisible godhead and
a Messiah to come and urged her to repent.
His words taking flight with the cries of centaurs
hiding in the forest, her mother a fallen
woman with shades of harlotry. Cover her
face with a veil, scatter ashes upon her head.
There will be a beating of wings: the angel
of death.

Salome was overcome, rejected by this
man and needed to protect her mother's name.
Salome was attractive, impressive
in her bearing, was asked by her father-in-
law to dance like a vision ecstatic,
the Dance of the Seven Veils, the erotic
Dance of the Seven Veils.

At first, she refused, supported by her mother
but Herod offered many gifts, enticements.
Salome would agree providing he would
grant her one wish and the wish, once granted will

be on oath. To this he agreed. The Dance
of the Seven Veils she performed and the veils
floated to earth. Herod asked what she wished.

I want the death of the prophet and what is
more, his head on a platter, a silver platter.
Then I will touch his hair, I will see close, his eyes,
and I will kiss his mouth.

Herod, no stranger to horror, said
this was outrageous and rejected this.
But Salome insisted on his oath. He
offered half his estate but she refused and
repeated the oath. Herod ultimately conceded
and had the prohet brought from the jail
and slain.

He was decapitated, the head placed on
a silver platter and brought to Salome
according to the oath. She then kissed the dead
prophet's lips.

Herod found this unbearable and ordered
the guards to put Salome to death, put down
by the sword for this atrocious act. And
there was a beating of wings, for the mystery
of love is greater than the mystery of
death.

ROME

In the beginning was the milk of wolves
nurturing the two, down the calendars
to Constantine and his conversion.
Touch and clasp the historic certainty,
grasp the legacy of Plato's form,
the ideal, the perfection thing.
The columns connect, the Hellenic debt.
And the Emperors: the good Aurelius
to Nero and those crucifixtions,
the Republic's assassinating blood.
The Centurian Guards stamp the road,
the chariots roll and the language comes.
Words resonate round the Forum.

In contrast, step out of togas
in public baths. The bodies drip.
They soak the flesh. The uniforms
(for all seasons, for all places) disrobe.
Today, Bellini's robust figures dominate
the fountains. Over the crowded Spanish steps,
Keat's place quietly looks down.
Through the facades of the so, so recent
eighteenth century, the ricketty buses
carry countless tourists to city landmarks.
And the Tiber still measurely moves
to the many outposts along the coast,
lapping the shores of the Middle Sea.

JULIUS CAESAR

In the play,
all those C's
(from Cicero to Claudius)
smeared with blood,
and the ensuing conflict
relentlessly macho,

wrangling
with daggers drawn.
No wonder,
the wife of Brutus
gives up the ghost
dying of a broken heart.

POMPEII

Below
the volcano,

unearth
the artifact,

road, bricks
and mortar,

the remains
skeletal.

The time's
encased:

reveal
an epoch,

venerate
a style,

resurrect
the cry

beneath
residuum.

HEROINE

Before the land
was ringed by garrisons
and those castles built
around the coast,

Gwenllian* was a lesser
known Boedicia,
another Joan of Arc
and what is more,
a mother of four.

She was a Welsh princess
who wrote of exploits,
chivalry, magic . . .
a confrontation
of one with rank,

aesthetic verve,
Celtic flair
and bravery.
Haunting is this
consummate woman:

the name, the deed
unparalleled.
In the 12th century
(engaging the Normans)
this teller of tales,

---

* Some scholars have attributed the Four Branches of the Mabinogi to her.

weaver of myths
was slain
on a battlefield
near Kidwelly
at the age of 38.

THE KEEP

In his gauntlet warmth
the sentinel stands
as cold as vigil,
squat as a stuffed owl,
his blade reflects
the vantage tower.

Within the keep,
they whirl and turn
to the flames merriment;
the cup is grasped
and raised in medieval ways.
Beyond, is the constant use

of wood, wind and water.
Oxen move sullen
in a mean furrow.
All peasants bow and scrape
in the manner borne.
All are held

in an ikon mould.
Beggars at the gate
cringe to the leper bell
and the figure squeezed
in the dungeon mouth
is ringed, condoned

by Latin prayers.
The dispersing mist
leaves no judgement
of the enemy within
or the gates without;
only the gargoyle's visage

scorns such yielding ignorance.

THE TRIBE

Deep in the forest
somewhere between Laos
and Thailand,
live a gentle people
the Mrabi tribe.

Like true animists
they propitiate (aware
of the spirit of leaves)
the essence of things
in simple ways,

relating, conjoining.
Beneath the canopy,
the forest envelopes them
in a womb of thick
bamboo trees to shade.

They eat the shoots
(the seeds medicinal)
and gouge out
the bigger stems
for drinking vessels.

The thin pipes make music
and other layers
woven to baskets
carrying fruit and grain.
Nocturnally,

to keep the beasts at bay
they guard themselves
with encircling flames:
the men on the outer rim
mother and child within.

Nomadically,
they move through forests
a sharing band
a simple endurance
traversing Rousseau's ideal.

POLYNESIAN

Those isles
like floating
emeralds
sprinked on to blue

with taboo
tattoo:
oceanic . . .
volcanic . . .
Pacific.

    A spear
    thrust to
    grass skirted
    dancing:
    coconut,

                  bread fruit
                  and yam.
                  A meteor
                  strikes in
                  vastness.

    Under
    the stars,
    we believe
    the sunset
    is where we

have come from.
The sunrise
is where
we are
going to.

WINCHESTER COLLEGE,*

the first boarding school for scholars
learning Latin and Greek, founded before
Agincourt with just seventy pupils.
There were commoners too, fee paying
for tuition and all preparatory
to their entry to the new college
at Oxford. Renowned for its moral
fervour since Chauser's time, yet there were riots

in Napoleonic days: the food was bad,
and the treatment harsh. Still, there were cloisters,
scrubbed tables, stained glass. The flint walls look as sharp
as when they were put up. In the hols.,
rooms are emptied of character and noise.
From time to time, the curriculum is stirred
by the perspective of a helicopter
singularly hovering far above.

* Founded by Wykeham in 1382.

VENICE

Is there anything new

to say about this city
with its stock images

of gondola, glass and mask?
To the notes
of a cafe quartette,

the trippers spill out
amongst the pigeons
of San Marco.
Despite

the tourist trance,
this place
has not lost its charm,
its theatrical backdrop.
Those mooring markers

still stick up
like colourful barber poles;
against the peeling facades,
each alleyway, each canal
has haunting vistas.
There are shadows

like the ghetto
and the Doge prison
where Casanova sulked.

Yet the strangest thing
is the unseen horse,
the unseen car
for all movement

is by water
or on foot.
And all this
because of a lagoon
unreal and out of time.
As I write this,
I am beginning to see
why Peggy Guggenheim*

chose to be buried here.

* American collector of modern art.

LANDING

To come to shores
where no men strayed before
these two who staked on mutiny,
the wretched crime.
Captain Dampier,* voyager
had them cast off
and left them stranded
on the southern isle.
For them to see that sail
fade terribly
and find a coast
bereft of man
where stones were cooled
by writhing snakes,
where earth is stricken
in a scorpion sting,
survival buried
in a larvae heep.
Like emus

hold their tiny heads
above the sand
grotesquelly stand
on land untrammeled
by the fierce quadruped.

---

* In the late 17th century, William Dampier, a pirate-mariner, put ashore two of his crew for attempted mutiny. They rowed to a desert island, later charted as Western Australia.

Who could dominate
a desert waste like this;
a burnt terrain
abandoned and succumbed,
beached as pebbles,
bleached to the bone?
Like leeches suck
where no blood circulates.
Escarpment scratched
ignited by the sun.
Stretched
where no language intervenes,
where tongues are stilled
licking a vast expanse.

FLORENTINE

I am out
of my depth

here
in Florence,

The gallery bursting
with Roman heads

and the paintings
tell of genius,

the bridge
with shops each side

in medieval style,
the voices operatic.

The facades ochre soft,
gently detailed.

(We need to know
the best endures).

And the Arno,
that natural constant:

is to believe
in water

as reliable
as the seagulls

pliably landing
on sandbanks.

INVENTOR

Going up
in a Tristar
(such a Wellsian
name for a plane)
the three engines heavily
confident in their thrust,
the thrust that Whittle dreamed:

> making things
> observable
> in a way
> the world
> had never seen
>
> watching rivers
> worm to the sea,
> crossing ranges
> like crusty loaves
> beneath your gaze
>
> making things
> navigable
> in a way
> explorers
> had always seen.

All distance
melts to horizons.
On the fuselage
of each jet plane,

there should be
a plaque to him
recognising the thrust

that he conceived.
A name to be recorded
in our time
with the Wright brothers,
Marconi,
Daimler-Benz
and Baird.

VULCAN

He was a true professional,*
a geologist fascinated
by the plutonic
(volcanoes being
his speciality).

Dedicated, recording
with such detail
the time scale,
the igneous glow, the magma
smouldering down there.

Such outpourings
predate the metamorphic,
the mere sedimentary:
an ambivalent godhead,
unpredictable, awesome.

With expertise,
he was always out there,
the location exotic,
elevated
like the Andes

to look down
at a sulphorous mass.

---

* Geoffrey Brown, age 49, a renowned geophycist perished on the Galeras volcano in Colombia on the 14th January 1993.

He knew, those who court
danger, unwittingly kiss
death: the obliteration

changing anything
to nothing
where disfuguration
has no meaning,
a mere eruption.

FORECAST: CONSTANT

There will be
    a turning
    from shade to light,

        eyes opening
        to horizons

        and ranges
        penetrating clouds.

There will be
    a glacial
    scraping of slopes,

        ice floes
        drifting . . . melting . . .

        and monsoons
        pelting the ground.

There will be
    winds howling
    in Siberian vastness,

        ominous tremors
        beneath the crust

        and occasionally,
        a volcanic sound.

There will be
> sand storms
> in torrid deserts,
>
> flooding
> in deep caverns
>
> and rivers
> oceanic.

There will be
> rain
> nurturing the land,
>
> branches swaying
> in tropic warmth
>
> and icebergs
> bearing south.

There will be
> a turning
> from light to shade,
>
> eyes closing
> sensing the dusk,
>
> a golden moon
> circled in blue
>
> and stars
> brilliant in dark.

VILLAGE

India
is a village
revolving
   in a water wheel
   sacred in those many
   fateful eyes.
Days are shaded
weaving in and out
of heart and hut.
   Laughter rings
   the child, innocent
   of books and scribes.
Seduced
by heat and wind.
women walk upright
   folding their lives
   in grace
   to the well
and the water wade.
The passion of the bride
will bare the burden
   until the monsoon
   brings forth
   fruit again.
The old man
in his wrinkled brow
conjures dancers

   down from Shiva.
   An image blurred
   on a cruel sun

is left to die
in the grey time.
Rice treks slump
   bodies in sweat
   barefoot
   in a water choke
of mud, close
to the scratch
and the pig squeal.
   From the crouch
   below the daub,
   a Guru seeks
the still centre
between the famine
and the wing crush
   of locusts.
   A potter prays in clay
   putting water to lips
through the long day
as old as stone age.
And the cattle move
   in priviliged ways
   as India
   is a village

revolving . . .

CO-ORDINATES

On the pier
people watch
for the wrinkled
tide to come;
while in the bay
a steamer waits
for the rising cone.
On the pier
they stand on planks

with gaps that go
straight down
to girder's rust,
seaweed black,
waves where walls
are lunar stone.
On the wing
seagulls snatch,
hover . . .

till the rope's
thrown free.
Drawn to the very end
passengers disembark.
At this point,
voyagers, watchers
meet, relate
on the worn steps
of the old pier.

NURSERY LINES

Baa baa black sheep
why are you forlorn?
Ding dong bell
you never can tell
for Little Jack Horner
is not in his corner.

Little Bo Beep
could not get to sleep
for Jack and Jill
were still up the hill
and the Hush-a-Bye Baby
dare not look down.

Simple Simon
was really a spyman
and Little Miss Muffet
learnt how to rough it
and Old Mother Hubbard
was truly lumbered.

Hickery Dickery Dock
the shepherd lost his flock
but found the Old Woman
who walked with no shoes.
Polly put the kettle on
as she ran out of booze.

The three little piggies
were sold at the stall
then incey wincey spinder

parachuted down
to see Humpty Dumpty
still on the wall.

When the three blind mice
came scurrying round,
Mary, Mary quite contrary
was usually left alone
while the Queen of Hearts
burnt her tarts and laughed.

HIDE AND SEEK,

is just a game
to find the hidden one.
You do not want
to be seen, to be caught
as an outsider,
out there alone.
Yet, excitement
was the thing.

Indoors, touching
wood in wardrobes,
fur brushing your face
and below stairs
that mix of leather
and carbolic.
Here, the small is large
diminishing

as in a black hole
feeling more snug
than the safest pearl.
Outdoors:
a mountain hide,
a fugitive
in ferns, safely
camouflaged

like a fox head
to teach me
a thing or two.

Then the large
seemed close,
a healthy smell
of grass making
excitement good.

CARAVAN*

In warm winds,
in heat and dust
the palms sway
in this waste
of burning sand
this passage
with camels burdened:
the caravan moves on.

Black veiled
hidden days of Egypt's
pious millions.
Elders clad
in dreary garments,
speechless maidens
stare in wonder:
the caravan moves on.

The desert's young
barefoot, puzzled;
languid victims
begging, starving.
The day eclipsed
by darker tombs.
On Egypt's endless
ancient wanderings:
the caravan moves on.

* Egypt 1944.

MEETING

I knew his face
yet it was thirty years
since our days
at school.

We had a drink
in the nearest bar—
in Guildford,
of all places.

In some way,
I resented his disregard
of the bourgeois
box of bricks.

> Royal Navy 43,
> signed on for five
> and seven and then
> the Merchant.

> Remember Turner,
> wore glasses,
> died of meningitis
> early in the war.

Thinking back
trying names
and placing,
tracing faces.

Williams
he's a dentist,
country house
a Volvo car.

The more we talked
the more unreal
were the moments
at the bar.

But that little
we had in common
glared under
hardened caps.

He was hedonistic
(easy come, easy go)
and whatever
he had not gathered

or became,
he was lively,
loquacious, generous . . .
I wondered then

which words will spring
to sum up me?

HEATHERBANK 1896*

From this house
you went by horse and trap
(cars were an idea
in Daimler's mind).
The house was built
before Victoria died,
her son shot grouse
in casino style.
At every time, there is need
of shelter from wind and rain,
for warmth and light
and that choice of site.
From foundation to elevation
   a building is an expression
   of its time. There are two
   staircases here: an upstairs,
   downstairs feature. From over
   the border, a distiller built
   this house. His name was Dewar.
Events overtook this house—
events overtake every house—
like the Relief of Mafeking
or that singular flight
across the Channel.
Then the Titanic sinks
and not long after, those unreturned
from those fields of pain.

---

* In Hindhead, Surrey: the home of Marie Stopes
  (1929-33).

And don't forget the silent screen.
Then the League of Nations
and the flapper years.
The radio is in every home
with Lady be Good, the Charleston
and What will I do?
Then the talkies highlight the stars,
the Spanish Civil War, Guernica
and the abdication notorious.
Searchlights criss cross the sky.
Barrage balloons bulge for Luftwaffe.
There were Dunkirk beaches, Normandy
landings and those depraved camps.
   Then the United Nations
and a television screen.
The car is dominant—
think of all that mobility!
Redundant are the stables
in front of Heatherbank
right up to the computer dream.
So touch these walls with grace
for they abide and take in
a century of change. The tiles
will shift in time and bricks
will weather but the tower's folly
wants to talk of endurance
what it is to survive.

THE HAILSTONES

It was the courtyard
of the hotel
(the dining room part
open to the sky).
We were into
the main course.
Then an enormous
clap of thunder.
It pelted down.
There was a flurry
of tables moving . . .
The waiter said

they hadn't seen
anything like it!
A forming through
air . . . hardening . . .
punishing us
(the exposed ones)
in sybaritic ease?
This sudden coming
was a translucent
jest by Pluvius*
like playful marbles
falling from heaven.

---

* Roman god of rain.

RECORDED*

The celebratory
voice of jazz

will always
be with us
in those grooves,

these tapes
and into
the waves

of Billie's
sad, sad
undertow

or the rounded,
assured tone
of Ella

and on to
that lingering phrase
by Sarah.

---

* Ella Fitzgerald died today: Saturday 15th June, 1996.

SAN MICHELE

Some imagine their dream house,
the dimensions, its location,
the panoramic view.
Few achieve their dream house;
Axel Munthe* did.
First was the vista,
high up in Anacapri.
The villa was built

with balcony next to
a dramatic cliff edge:
the drop precipitous,
impressive elevation.
The interior walls white,
so, precisely place
the Roman fragment . . .
ceramic . . . mosaic . . .

The old chapel,
adjacent,
converted to a chamber
for the grand piano
and recital staged.
The garden cloistered:
water trickled rocks,
birds' falsetto notes
and bouganvilia, vines,

---

* A Swedish doctor (1857-1949), who practiced in Paris and Rome. As a young man, was fascinated with this site in Capri. It became his lifetime endeavour.

hibiscus, oleander . . .
Like paradisiac moulds,
the sculptures neatly placed.
As revelatory as a gallery,
a place to walk through
(an integral mode,
organic, complete).
Charmed, reach out to touch

and share in his ideal,
embodiment of a dream.

AN ART DECO SHOP

There should be music
by Rodgers
and words by Hart.

> There is a golden horn,
> tiny needles
> for those waxed grooves.

There are chrome lights
(indirect on walls)
so sensually hung.

> There are glass rigged
> yachts and marble tops,
> ultra radios with knobs on.

There are tiles in black,
a Legér print,
both cubistically apt.

> There are figurines
> in butterfly poses
> and multi-coloured shades.

There are imbedded
images frozen
in Lalique glass.

> There are cigarette lighters
> for the Passing Cloud
> in the long, long grasp.

There are photographs
of Tallulah,
Dietrich and Louise Brooks.

    There are soda syphons,
    a cocktail shaker
    to lace the iced glass.

There is a neon sign
for this hedonic style.
When the Depression starts . . .

    there should be notes
    by Beiderbecke,
    lyrics by Cole-Porter . . .

MOVIES

I came across
these cigarette cards,
with portraits
of move stars;
    autographed
    in each corner
    and on the writing side:
    born in Nebraska
the wide expanse
of the U.S.A.
Slip down the years
to studio guards,
    western palaces
    where dreams
    were richly made.
    Turn back the cards
to neon signs,
posters brash
and carpets soft.
Each decade
    gave us names
    like W. C. Fields,
    Gable, Crawford . . .
    and on the walls
pictures hung
of Myrna Loy, Tracy
and Franchote Tone.
A few stars died

>   before the film
>   was canned:
>   a Robert Walker
>   or Thelma Todd.
> There were faces
> in supporting roles,
> always remembered
> but never named;
>   and many a moll
>   of a gangster mob
>   touched a cold,
>   white screen.
> The preamble always
> with company names:
> Paramount, Metro
> Warner and Fox.
>   Alice Fay numbers,
>   an epic of Ghengis Khan
>   all came out
>   on that magic beam:
>
> the Hollywood dream.

LIMELIGHT

For some with stagy,
seductive names
like Jean Harlow,
 Carol Lombard,
 Thelma Todd,
 Carol Landis,
 Carmen Miranda,
 Marilyn Monroe . . .
the studio lights
went out and never
came back on.

SATURNALIA

Accordions drawn
in old arcades,
a gaslight plays
shadows on
erratic shades.
Expectant night
when fairy lights
warm the sky.
The crowd holds on
to chairoplanes.
The organ strain
pulsates

punctuates the air.
The pub inhales,
sweats the night away.
Like tom-cats fight
break at the seam,
sag and fall apart.
For a little time,
dullness evaporates.
The whirring stops.
Lights are doused:
another Saturday
fades.

CROWD

With upright stance,
the baboons squeal
and pounce, shrink
into night
and the tidal bore
of crowds.
Faces pace
the pavement, pouring

in and round
the town;
the bull fight
we do not approve,
merely the thing
that's done.
Only the turnstile
marks our singularity.

Above the throng,
the park's calm
sculpture dance.
And on the cold,
rough stone,
watch the spider
breathe design
in solitude.

METROPOLIS III

They roam the city centre
drinking and forgetting
fearful of the morrow;

their steps perfunctory,
puerile is the laughter.
They dominate the streets

like night marauders
lurching on a drab set
stained with dross.

The backdrop: empty shops
waiting for a new lease,
a loan, some sort of uplift.

Cheap and oily phrases
drip from tabloids
and from the top shelf

venal phantasies look down.
Engines grind and groan,
violate the air or clog

the arteries to languish
in a concrete parking lot.
With a prolonged howl

and ambulance passes.
Overhead, seagulls squawk,
wheel for the shore.

METROPOLIS IV

The Ramblas* is a pedestrian
zone graced by some old trees.
Traffic moves right or left
leaving the central area free.
People are drawn to this avenue
(the shops modishly cosmopolitan)
where they parade defying
the traffic density.
Antlike in their movement,
they are a considerate crowd
avoiding each other with ease.

The new art gallery
contrasts with spaciousness,
a whiteness promoting quietude
with a poised, human feel.
Like an insect flow,
one artist sees people
following one another
in a fixed parade.

Adjustment is a virtue.
The last thing you want
in Barcelona is a car.

Like steel chariots
they move up and down
across grid avenues

---

* In Barcelona with a population density next to Calcutta.

and manic in intent
are those rasping bikes.
(One solution is to go
underground in linear
style, a termite zone:
concepto Metro).
Fortunately,
the pedestrian crossings

are effectively wide
separating the machine
from the human being.
And all automatically
controlled by red
and green lights,
for the ultimate
sound of the city
is the siren
furiously
pressing the air.

STILL LIFE

In Madrid,
this gallery* was so impressive
the walls graced
by painting's magnificence:
the names quintessential
from concrete to abstract,
surreal and actual.
The still life eye of fish
glistening

a silver coated sardine.
And in the mercado
slabs displaying
marble red cuts
of sharks snatched
from the lapping green.
On the bus back,
I glanced
as we overtook

a lorry double-decked
with cargo exposed
(a live stock haul)
the pigs munching
still making them fat
ready for the drop.
That painting by Bacon
swilled on my eyes,
swirled in my mind.

* Thyssen museo.

ALMS

The first was an old woman
with palm held out,
aptly garbed in black.
Small boned, precisely
contained like a cat.
A model for Manet,
too theatrical, perhaps.

The second was young
selling La Farola,*
confident, proclamatory,
sustained with anger.
This is protestation!
The pesetas were conditional.
Dignity showed through.

The third was customary.
A beggar, garrish T-shirt.
A nice turned on smile,
knowingly with plastic
cup in hand like
a street stoic resigned
to indifference.

The last played a guitar
(unconcerned with coins
in the upturned cap)
fingered the taut strings
with a certain panache.
The music was classical.
Irresistible!

* The magazine sold in Spain by the unemployed.
  Trans: lantern.

BUSKERS

Breathe sharpened,
vapourized
that shopping day
(just before Xmas)
when the clear notes
merged
half way down
the High Street.
At one end,
a solitary jazz
saxophonist,

at the other,
a brass ring
of Salvationists
complimenting
each other
like instrumental,
festive book ends:
a sensual,
singular tone
in a circle
of witnesses.

ONE IS A LONELY NUMBER

With a crude discordance,
he plays the mouth organ
like notes
for the inarticulate.
In a slovenly way,

the cardboard is put down
for the few coins
tolerating the endless clatter
of feet on dull pavements,
complimenting

his squalid digs
where there are no illusions.
It would be better
to be a Buddhist monk
handing out the bowl

resignedly
on higher slopes
where there is another perspective
different from this High Street
with its flat extensions.

CERTAINTY

None of them
are teaching now,

is one thing
you can be sure of.

Outside,
we stood or sat,

assembled in front
of the moving camera.

It is the college
photograph

(the panoramic kind)
to be unfolded

many times
like a scroll.

Nostalgia
is a fading notion

as remote
as a scratch

on a board that's black
or the feel of papyrus.

CO
OP

White as the milk
it carries,
the electric float
is driven by a woman
tightly styled in corduroy:
a modern Owenite,
each delivery
rounded with a smile.

Behind her
fields stretch out
dotted with eyes
oval and dark
and from them
a lowing is scored
like an overture
to millennium.

PREFERENCE*

If you can accept
an early false start
when a pine marten
tampers with the car's
wiring or the screeching
of buzzards swooping . . .
you might like it here.

If you like isolation,
holes in the floorboards,
death watch beetles,
the hooting of owls
(at three in the morning)
and that nightingale sound . . .
you might like it here.

If you don't mind
frogs tripping you up
there on their path,
dragon flies burring,
the mooing of cows
or the meowing of cats . . .
you might like it here.

If you want to sit
with bleating goats
there with the sun
incredibly close,
or wade crotch high
through abundant snow . . .
you might like it here.

* Based on a letter from a friend.

CIAO

Up,
up and away
in my glitzy balloon.
As light as a party hat,
as blue as a tropic lagoon.
Nothing succeeds like excess.
V   e   r   s   a   c   i.*
As gay as a bauble
as bright as
the moon.
A
  r
   r
    i
     v
      e
       d
        e
         r
          c
           i

* The fashion designer was murdered at Miami Beach on July 15th, 1997.

SNAP

Fixed through light
in darkness,
every picture taken
has its negative side.
    The image caught
    will be reproduced,
    circulated
    and transmitted
for the many eyes
to gaze upon.
(It seems they have
a proprietary claim,

    as if a part
    of you belonged
    to them!)
    In the blaze
of fame, a shadow
falls on vanity
for with each clicking
a bit of you
    is taken away,
    by an evil eye,
    as some tribal
    folk believe.

Utility

H e avy
s mooth
g l ass
stopper.
Perfect
f i t.

This is
n e c k
this is
s h ape
this is
s mooth
transparency.
This vessel is
more like a decanter
or carafe of wine. Yes,
it is fermented, diluted
this acid made from grape
poised (the vinegar contained)
down to the round and shapely base.

```
         r  e
      b     l
    m         l
  U             a
```
Furled
and unextended
is collapsible, portable
or macho, swordlike. Yet pressed
open, taut, functional, sculptured
and protective. Cupped and curved the
shape is feminine. A tense piece of sprung
engineering as integrated as a toadstool ready
for the rain or on a summer day, a parasol to shade
the rays

r
i
g
i
d
l
y

h
e
l
d

i
n

p
l
a
c
e

CRESSIDA

'Joy's soul lies in the doing'*

And Cressida
what it is to be a woman,

a dangling fruit
prised unreservedly.
Drawn to the difference

the other gender: the assurity,
the grasp of props, the outer things.
They stride the stage with swords,
with armour, a destructive

or protective shield.
This is the state of soldiery,
the ribbons of honour,
camaradarie.
Creative is the inner blood

unlike those combative wounds.
So perform in arclight,
draw power to oneself
central to the artifice
(the wanton liaison,
a disloyal wench).

To be carried
on the rapids so far

---

* Shakespeare.

from the masculine edge
to be alone and dream
of archetypes: a Cleopatra
mercurial, the make-up
and the feline eyes;

a Sheba ambivalent
with bangles of diplomacy,
or Delilah
in dress diaphonous,
the deceptive mirror,
and Helen, sculptured:
a symmetric reason for war.
And the fountains leap

bursting here, there
and everywhere.

NOT MERELY BEING, BECOMING

A bosoming beatitude
is the first day
of Summer,
when women blossom
in bright blouses
billowing skirts
bursting out
of the merely fashionable
blissfully blooming
becoming.

APHRODITE

Along peninsular,
when the moon
is high, she wades

>into sea spray;
>then waves of salt
>on Cyprus shore

to paddle foam.
I see the eyes,
fondle hair,

>kiss her lips,
>grasp the fingers,
>touch her nails,

hold the shoulders,
embrace her shape.
The stone statute

>shows this frame:
>the head, the arms,
>legs and hands,

breast and waist
down thigh to feet.
Along this coast

>I kneel in awe
>on sand, beneath
>a lucid moon.

HOTEL ARIELE*

From the bedroom,
the window shutters
were appropriate;

the poplars pointed
and truly apt,
for this was Tuscany.

The skyline etched
by burnt tiles, chimneys.
A surface skin

of ochre are the walls.
The river just there
at the end of the road

that Dante saw
here in Florence.
And in this room,

we find each other,
she as Beatrice
in supple play

with my caressing
fondling
enshrines a body

* Air spirit or angel.

yielding.
Interior softness,
folds and rolls.

Lips osculate.
A figure wrapped,
a voluptuous map,

the epitome of love.
For this is paradise
and I write

inadequate
cantos to our love
in this room

of the Ariele.

ABSENCE

It is a duologue
in a mutual frame
absorbing responses,
revealing attitudes,
    theme exposing
    and with more contact
    other moods
    are set in train.
The focus is you:
to and fro
conversational.
And the intimate
    that relates
    to the beholden
    mirrors each other
    dependent on
making a whole.
Yet, when the one
is removed
as on a train
    departing,
    the absence accrues
    (persona and character
    have gone)
And there is a lack
so that the one
is more there
more aware

of a presence.

WAITRESS

Our train stopped at Basle
waiting for the Locarno train,
we had coffee in the station
dining room. Dexterously

balancing a tray, she glided
through that crowded room.
Laying the table, she gave
style to a menial task.

And with the smooth look
of porcelain, took the order.
(The ephemeral is mirrored
as a glacial shadow).

Today, she will be old,
if not gone, yet not
so long ago, she shone
like a golden moon
in a pale, blue sky.

IN THE TWINKLE OF AN EYE

A ballerina
firmly
poised
seen as
sculpture
in the moment.
Every
thing is
upright
held there
accentuated
vertical
like a minaret,
or notes
from high
to low
making
their sound,
their mark
on scores.
The rest
is time
extending
where it
occurs
along
a plane
for a moment
like words
on a page
arranged
to make
a shape
a point
in line
for eyes.

HAIKU

Proud as Picasso,
the symbolizing doves swoop
as in a fly-past.

The grouse are cared for
before the glorious twelfth's
salvo of cartridges.

On the roadside, sprays
are placed there, upright, in line
die with the victim.

Looking down on the Gobi,
from those barren heights,
alone is the snow leopard.

NAME DROPPING

And the reviewer said
that they were real poets.
And I said to myself,

who are the unreal poets?
Perhaps Caedmon
the Northumbrian cowherd,

or those Metaphysicals
with spiky images
or Leopardi's

sad cadence and Coleridge
lightly into laudanum
to Emily Dickinson

of the short stanza
(and less recognition)
or Mallarme's

symbolism
echoing anothers
move to obscurity;

on to the surreal
Apollinaire
and Sitwell's stylish

eccentricity
with Lawrence pounding
natural rhythms,

William Carlos Williams
and that animated
paper

with Borges
in his labyrinth
of mirrors

(and getting closer)
those direct Beatniks
like Corso,

Ferlinghetti
all unreal
revealing the reality

beneath
with Stevie Smith
on going, becoming

something other
like flowers
in unreal splendour.

SURREAL

I. I see
    the reason
    for the storm,

    where creatures
    adamantine
    spawn.

    The wind
    runs hair and scalp
    with sand.

    The shell
    on this languid
    shore is skull.

    The ledge
    abated with words
    relating

    to a cloud.

II. Like desert waste
    the pillows stretch.
    Lighter

    than counterpane
    you drift down
    and down the dunes.

The scorpion
claws the cacti
and the Dervish dance

white
around a camel skull.
Caught.

in window light
the frame
is rational

and the dream is gone.

INSTANTER

Below the books
and the white, blank wall
is the moment
where he felt no more
than a grain of sand.

Between the rainbow
and persistent rain
is the moment
where waves recoil
in a driving storm.

Behind the thinking
and a casual stroll
is the moment
when passion plays
a self tormenting jig.

Between the ritual
and a Bohemian dance
is the moment
when a frenzied eye
sees the broken glass.

Beneath the established
and the insistent truth
is the moment
a Tyndale hangs
for a pile of books.

Beyond the Buddha
and the stoic pride
is the moment
when his mind discards
a preconception.

Between a conscience
and an old confession
is the moment
that condemns the nature
from which we came.

Between the inspired
and the classic form
is the moment
integral
like ears of corn.

SCORE

Words
are so irrelevant
when expectancy
hangs
in concert halls:
strings and flutes
the air
with language
tapped
from scores;

battens
like a magic totem
fulfilling guests
with awe,
a sound
unparalleled
to quicken
the night
and the magnitude
of moons.

EXPRESSIVO

Expectancy
    conbrio
hangs
    amaroso
with reeds
    lamentoso
in concert
    moderato.
A language
    animato
tapped
    saltando
from scores
    fortissimo
quickens
    vivace.
The night
    andante
battens
    staccato
strings
    caloroso.
The air
    tremolo
the moon
    tranquillo
magnifies
    bravura
the meaning
    dolente
of words
    vibrato.

A fine
    bel canto
with chorus
    morendo
of notes
    tocatto
concerto
    largo.
The tempo
    veloce
symphonic
    scherzando.
Magic
    capriccioso
flutes
    pianissimo
sound
    appassionato
the closing
    presto
to final
    crescendo.

SILENCE

Beyond all sound
is each day's dawn:

from stalagmite
to rainbow arch

or lake becalmed
as ice compact,

extended ocean
to mountain pass

or heavy sculpture
cut from rock,

(those colours fixed
in stone or sand)

to sifted desert
still at dusk.

Then from a cloud
the moon emerges

symphonic pause
for a distant star

in the void extant.

PROSPECT

There
outside
the window
was the constancy
of trees.

Beyond,
were mountains
distant
in their own
time.

Above,
the stars
perspective
reels.

FIRMAMENT

Darkness comes
    with a starlit sky
    and I am overcome
  by this galaxy
    in orbiting place.
        An outer-inner tension
keeps it there.
  Each point of light
    was seen by Chaldean eyes
    naming configurations
      picked out before familiar
  Grecian, godlike names.
  Our spiral galaxy
spreads out

    with light years between
like Orion
with a star
    a hundred times larger
than the sun.
    All distance breached
      by the long-eyed glass
        and a cosmic edge touched only
      by those radio waves.
As a child,
    Galileo Galilei
  was a magic name
for me:
    that controversial telescope!

My father
   tried to describe
            the enormity of space,
   and I still think
   of grains of sand
      filling a large room,
   each grain a star
making up
   the Milky Way.
           Then turn to other galaxies
      with a similar scale
yet each grain
        this time is a galaxy
     filling the same room,

     to make the universe.
I am told,
        one galaxy passes through another
   and nothing touches.
     There is no collision
        for there are light years of space
between.
   I think of this
     looking at the sky
        a privileged observer
      by courtesy of a star
        another of those points of light
    seemingly shining
   for you and me?

PYRE

You can be sure
this is a place
of no fear, no pain.

The mourners know
they are in
a fragile frame,

relate to the peace
absolute and the purity
of an egalitarian flame.

You can be sure
this is a place
for flowers displayed.

For the one
is without and rests
in memory's continuum,

to be at one
with the highest cloud
and the deepest cave.

ADJURATION

Disperse
my ashes there
on the verge
of the Golden Valley.*
And I will be

with the rabbits
in their burrows
mating
making each other.
And they will surface

to the sun
and the soft grass
crouching, munching
(despite the shadow
of fox, of gun

and the disease
that put them down).
They are content,
contained and glad
of their lot.

* Hindhead.

RECURRENCE*

    I see
  this sparking
  confluence
somewhere between
Mars and Jupiter;

to be seen again
  (by other eyes)
    in about six
      thousand years
    time.

* Halle-Bopp comet; April 3, 1997.

SOLAR

The long night
attends each galaxy.
It must be enough
that we should be
for this brief time
revolving
then be resolved
with each exploding star.

HIDE AND SEEK